A Night at the Symphony

Stories of Great Orchestral Works
with Early Intermediate to Intermediate Piano Arrangements

Bernadine Johnson & Carol Matz

A Night at the Symphony takes piano students on a fascinating journey into the exciting world of orchestral music. The book presents music and information from some of the most beloved orchestral works in history. Along with early-intermediate to intermediate piano arrangements of favorite orchestral themes, it includes instructions for organizing a symphony-themed recital, information on the basics of the orchestra, an explanation of symphonic terms, highlights of orchestral history and more.

Seven timeless orchestral pieces are explored. The section on each piece includes:

- **a piano arrangement by Carol Matz**
- **interesting background information on the composition and its form**
- **a biography of the composer**
- **a fun activity page**

Dedications:

To my boys—Josh, Jeff and Jonathan—for having to endure the constant quizzing of classical music in the car.

Bernadine Johnson

To my mom, Judith Matz, who has the uncanny ability to hum any theme from any symphony, beginning to end!

Carol Matz

Cover art: Historical engraving of Franz Liszt (1811–1886) conducting an orchestra. Colorization by Sarah Lewis
Interior art: Courtesy of *Digital Stock, Dover Publications, Dynamic Graphics, EyeWire* and *Planet Art.*

Table of Contents

To the Teacher

How to Create *A Night at the Symphony*

Instructions for Organizing a Symphony-Themed Recital

This book can be used to present a theme recital that combines piano performance with interesting information about the symphonic repertoire that is featured. This can be a creative and fun way to involve students of all ages and ability levels from your studio.

Before the program

1. Choose the repertoire to present from this book.

2. Assign everyone in your studio a specific duty: presenting background information, piano performance, handing out programs, welcoming guests to the recital, helping with publicity, refreshments, setup or cleanup.

3. Have a dress rehearsal at the performance facility so that the students become familiar with the piano, the microphone (if used), where to stand, etc.

4. Contact local newspapers for coverage of the event.

Optional idea:

Consider combining students on multiple keyboards, including synthesizers and digital keyboards. Also, consider using a student conductor to give the feeling of a "keyboard orchestra."

The program

1. Select students to pass out programs at the door.

2. Have a recording of symphonic music playing in the background as guests arrive.

3. Begin the program with some highlights of symphonic history (see pages 12–13).

4. Present each selection as follows: a description of the form, interesting facts about the piece, the composer's biography, and the performance of the selection.

5. Encourage students to "dress up" to give the evening a special elegance.

After the program

1. Serve elegant refreshments: sparkling punch, a variety of cookies, petit four cakes, hors d'oeuvres.

2. Submit a videotape of the program to your local cable television station. (Check with the station to be sure you are not violating copyright laws.)

Orchestra Basics

What is an orchestra?

An orchestra is a large group of musicians who play music together.

What is a symphony?

A symphony is a long composition for orchestra, usually with three or four movements (sections). Each movement varies in mood, tempo or style.

Where do the words "orchestra" and "symphony" come from?

They are both ancient Greek words. The word "orchestra" originally referred to the section of the theater between the stage where the musicians performed and the audience. "Symphony" means "sounding together."

What is a symphony orchestra?

A large orchestra that plays classical music is usually called a "symphony orchestra," even though it may play other forms of music in addition to symphonies.

Are all orchestras the same size?

The size of an orchestra is usually determined by the type of music it is performing. The number of musicians in an orchestra may change from one piece to the next. While orchestras of the 1700s only used about 30 players, some orchestral compositions written today can use over 100 musicians.

What is a concertmaster?

A concertmaster is the best violinist in the orchestra. He or she usually gets to play the solo parts and leads the final tuning of the orchestra.

Is a piano ever used in the orchestra?

Yes. In a piano concerto (a piece written for orchestra and piano soloist), a grand piano will appear onstage. Pianos are also sometimes used with other symphonic repertoire to add color and texture to the music.

Are other types of keyboard instruments ever used in an orchestra?

A harpsichord can be used for music that was composed before 1750 (from the Baroque era). Electronic keyboards are sometimes used in modern music. Another keyboard instrument called a celesta is used in the famous *Dance of the Sugar-Plum Fairy* from Tchaikovsky's *The Nutcracker*. The organ has been used in some orchestral music, such as Saint-Saëns's Third Symphony.

What is the seating arrangement of the musicians?

Musicians are seated in four sections: strings, woodwinds, brass and percussion. (See chart below.)

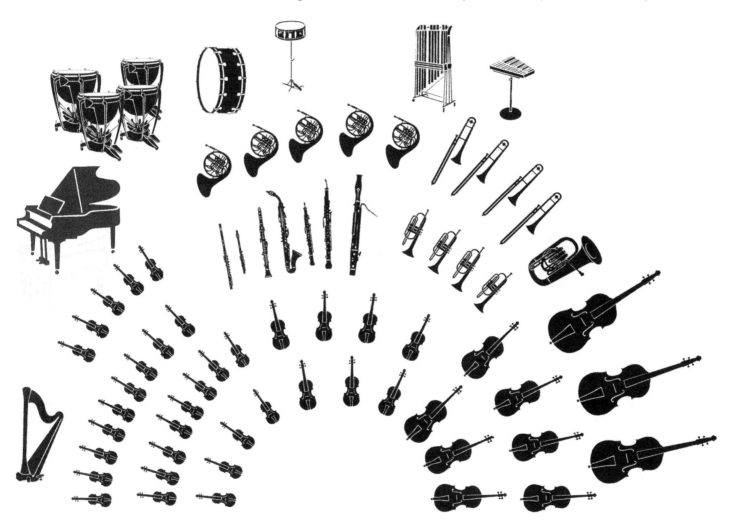

The Sections of the Orchestra

The poem below will help you understand the four main sections of the orchestra.

The violin (who often gets
To play the melody),
Viola, cello, bass and harp
Make up the string fam'ly.

The oboe, flute and clarinet,
Bassoon and piccolo
Make up the woodwind section
And the English horn, also.

The brass can be quite powerful.
They blow some mighty tones.
This section has the trumpets, tubas,
French horns and trombones.

Percussion sections have the drums,
The cymbals, bells and gong.
The wood blocks, chimes and xylophone,
And many more belong.

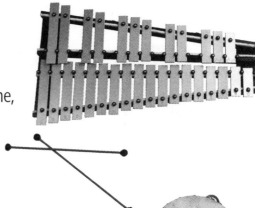

The strings are seated in the front,
Quite easy to be seen.
Brass and percussion in the back,
The winds are in-between.

The conductor leads the orchestra.
They watch each move he makes.
Musicians keep their eyes on him
So they won't make mistakes.

The Conductor

What is the history of conducting?

In ancient Greek theater, dancers were coordinated by somebody stamping on the ground. In medieval churches, hand signals were used for the melodic line. Early orchestras were led by a musicians who played while standing, so directions could be seen by all.

Why does a conductor move his arms?

In general, the right arm conducts the tempo and meter. The left arm gives the signals to make the music expressive, and to remind musicians when to enter.

Does the conductor only use his arms?

No. The musicians will also be watching the conductor's face and the movements of his body.

What does a conductor need to know?

The conductor needs to be a very skilled musician with a good knowledge of how every instrument works. He must have the ability to sight-read in all clefs, to practically memorize the entire composition he'll be conducting, and to familiarize himself with every instrumental part. The conductor must also know how to communicate musical ideas, not only verbally at rehearsals, but also through body movements during a performance.

What are some of the conductor's additional responsibilities?

It is the conductor's job to choose the orchestra's music and decide how it will be played. He is also responsible for leading rehearsals, choosing guest soloists, assisting in auditions for the orchestra, and helping section leaders with problems.

What is the name of the stick that a conductor uses?

A baton. In the 15th century, conductors used a roll of music to conduct. In the 17th century, they used a heavy stick to pound on the floor. Leonard Spohr (1784–1859), a German composer and conductor, was the first to use a baton.

Who are some important conductors today?

Vladimir Ashkenazy, James Conlon, Keith Lockhart, Zubin Mehta and John Williams.

Symphonic History (in Song)

The melodies that follow are taken from music that you will study later in the book. The words to the melodies answer questions that relate to the history of symphonic music.

Practice directions: • First, play the melody with the correct fingerings.
• Then sing the words as you play the melody.

Who wrote over 500 concertos for orchestra?

Spring (from *The Four Seasons*)   Antonio Vivaldi

It was-n't Mo-zart or Bach, Hay-dn, Tchai-kov-sky or Bar-tók. It was An-ton-ni-o Vi-val-di. He was a Bar-oque com-po-ser, the "Fa-ther of the Con-cer-to," the Red Priest from Ve-nice_ It-a-ly.

Where does the word "serenade" come from?

Eine Kleine Nachtmusik   Wolfgang Amadeus Mozart

It all start-ed out in It-a-ly sing-ing songs out in the night, you see. "Se-ra"____ is an I-tal-ian word____ (in case you have-n't heard).____ "Eve-ning" is what it means_ in It-a-ly. A ser-e-nade is a lit-tle night mu-sic song.

Who is called the "Father of the Symphony"?

Theme from the "Surprise" Symphony

Franz Joseph Haydn

Hay - dn is the one they call "Fa - ther of the Sym - pho - ny." Wrote one hun - dred (plus a few) and his form changed mu - sic his - to - ry.

Who is the first composer to add a chorus to a symphony?

Theme from Symphony No. 5

Ludwig van Beethoven

Bee - tho - ven did! Bee - tho - ven did! He did some - thing no - bod - y else had e - ver tried. He wrote a sym - pho - ny with "Ode to Joy" in - side. In "Num - ber Nine" for the first time a cho - rus sings. It's fine!

10

What is a "suite"?

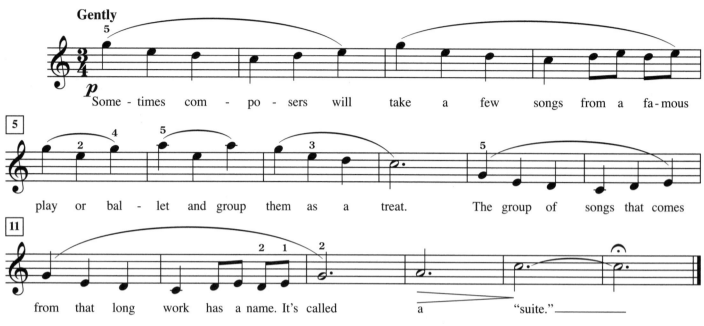

Who are some famous composers of symphonies?

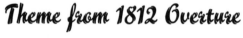

Who was the first composer to mix classical music with jazz?

Themes from "Rhapsody in Blue™"

George Gershwin

Moderately

f
It was on Feb - ru - ar - y twelfth in nine - teen - twen - ty - four.__ It had nev -

3
er been done__ be - fore. It was George Gersh - win *f*

5
who mixed sym - pho - nic sound with jazz. *rit.* Yeah! *ff*

Highlights of Orchestral History

950 B.C.–900 A.D.

- Ancient orchestras are formed to celebrate public events, using instruments such as trumpets, harps, horns, pipes and percussion instruments.

1000–1599

- The first complete piece of music is printed in 1473.

- Kings, princes, towns and even ships create their own bands to provide music for special occasions.

1600s

- The first orchestras are developed when groups of strings and brass play for ballets and operas.

- Instrumental music develops and composers create many new orchestral forms, including the concerto for solo instrument and orchestra, and the symphony.

- Italian composer Jean-Baptiste Lully leads a large orchestra at the court of French King Louis XIV.

- In Italy, the *concerto grosso,* which uses a small group of solo instruments, is developed.

1700s

- Johann Sebastian Bach improves the technique of writing for the orchestra.

- Italian violinmaker Antonio Stradivari creates stringed instruments of unsurpassed tone quality.

- Concerts become more public and are no longer confined to churches, palaces and the ballrooms of the wealthy.

- The Mannheim (Germany) Orchestra becomes one of the musical wonders of Europe by emphasizing dynamics.

- Flutes, oboes, bassoons and clarinets are added to the orchestra.

- Composers, especially Haydn and Mozart, establish the main forms of orchestral music—the concerto and the symphony.

- Haydn develops the form of the four-movement symphony and becomes known as the "Father of the Symphony."

1800s

- The strong emotional quality of the music of Beethoven and Schubert ushers in the Romantic period.

Timeline of Important Events in Orchestral History

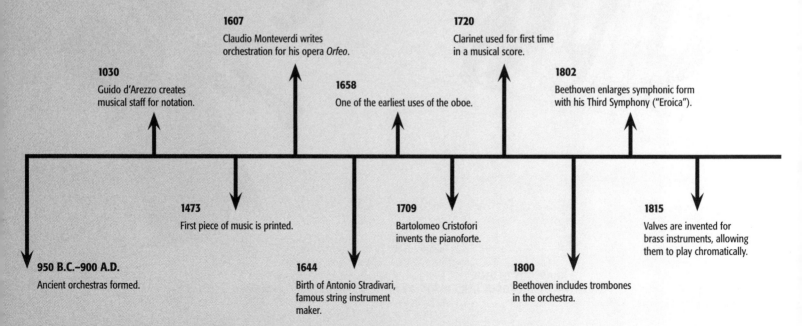

1030 Guido d'Arezzo creates musical staff for notation.

1607 Claudio Monteverdi writes orchestration for his opera *Orfeo.*

1658 One of the earliest uses of the oboe.

1720 Clarinet used for first time in a musical score.

1802 Beethoven enlarges symphonic form with his Third Symphony ("Eroica").

1473 First piece of music is printed.

1709 Bartolomeo Cristofori invents the pianoforte.

1815 Valves are invented for brass instruments, allowing them to play chromatically.

950 B.C.–900 A.D. Ancient orchestras formed.

1644 Birth of Antonio Stradivari, famous string instrument maker.

1800 Beethoven includes trombones in the orchestra.

- The percussion section, as well as individual instruments such as the harp, are added to the symphony orchestra.

- The orchestra expands to approximately 100 musicians, allowing composers to create a variety of new sounds.

- Conductors are added to the orchestra.

- Valves are added to brass instruments, allowing them to play chromatically.

- Symphonies increase to almost an hour in length.

- French composer Hector Berlioz introduces new instruments into the orchestra, such as the cornet and bass clarinet.

- "Program music," which suggests visual ideas, becomes increasingly popular.

- French composer Claude Debussy writes the orchestral piece *The Afternoon of a Faun,* establishing Impressionist orchestral music.

- Many new concert halls open and numerous orchestras are founded, including the Boston Symphony Orchestra, the Vienna Philharmonic and the Berlin Philharmonic.

1900s

- The first music to be broadcast on radio—Rossini's *William Tell*—is transmitted from New York.

- Improvements in sound recording encourage conductors to take their orchestras into the recording studio.

- American composer George Gershwin writes orchestral works that incorporate jazz and blues styles.

- The standard pitch of "A440" is adopted (440 vibrations per second for "A" above middle C). All orchestral instruments are tuned using this standard.

- Russian composer Sergei Prokofiev composes *Peter and the Wolf,* written for orchestra and narrator. In this work, characters in the story are "played" by different orchestral instruments.

- Composer Benjamin Britten composes *The Young Person's Guide to the Orchestra.*

- Composers begin adding electronic instruments to orchestral compositions.

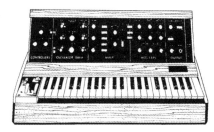

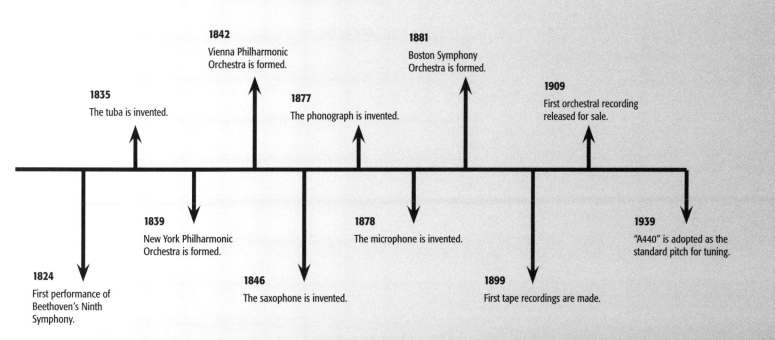

1824
First performance of Beethoven's Ninth Symphony.

1835
The tuba is invented.

1839
New York Philharmonic Orchestra is formed.

1842
Vienna Philharmonic Orchestra is formed.

1846
The saxophone is invented.

1877
The phonograph is invented.

1878
The microphone is invented.

1881
Boston Symphony Orchestra is formed.

1899
First tape recordings are made.

1909
First orchestral recording released for sale.

1939
"A440" is adopted as the standard pitch for tuning.

Spring

Concerto No. 1 in E Major
from "The Four Seasons"

Composer: **Antonio Vivaldi**

First Performed: **1725 in Italy**

Form: **Concerto**

About the Music

The Four Seasons, first published in Amsterdam in 1725, is one of Vivaldi's most famous works and one of the most often-heard pieces of classical music. During Vivaldi's lifetime, this composition was well-loved and performed throughout Europe. King Louis XV of France was very fond of the *Spring* concerto, and often requested that it be played.

The Four Seasons is a set of four concertos (*Spring, Summer, Fall, Winter*) written entirely for strings. Each concerto has three movements (fast–slow–fast), a favorite form of Vivaldi's. *The Four Seasons* is sometimes referred to as "program music"–a composition that tells a story or "paints" a picture. In the *Spring* concerto, you can hear the gentle sounds of birds and brooks, as well as a thunderstorm. The musicians play fast trills to imitate bird calls and running notes to reproduce the sound of running streams. Fast repeated notes and scales are used to represent the thunder and lightening of the spring storm.

Vivaldi included a short original poem at the beginning of each concerto in *The Four Seasons.*
Vivaldi's poem for *Spring* follows:

Springtime is upon us.
The birds celebrate her return with festive song,
and murmuring streams are softly caressed by the breezes.
Thunderstorms, those heralds of spring, roar,
casting their dark mantle over heaven.
Then they die away to silence,
and the birds take up their charming songs once more.
On the flower-strewn meadow,
with leafy branches rustling overhead,
the goatherd sleeps, his faithful dog beside him.
Led by the festive sound of rustic bagpipes,
nymphs and shepherds lightly dance
beneath the brilliant canopy of spring.

About the Form

CONCERTO

The word *concerto* means "performing together"—a combined effort by a variety of different performers. A concerto is often written for a soloist who plays along with the orchestra. However, many concertos of the 17th and 18th centuries are simply ensemble (group) pieces, without featuring one soloist. Vivaldi's *Spring* is this type of concerto, known as a *concerto grosso*, in which a small group of players is featured within the larger group.

About the Composer

ANTONIO VIVALDI (1678–1741)

Antonio Vivaldi, one of the greatest composers of the Baroque period, was born in Venice, Italy during an earthquake. Vivaldi became not only a great composer and violinist, but he was also a priest. He was nicknamed the "Red Priest" because of his bright red hair. After he left the priesthood, Vivaldi took a job teaching music at an orphanage for girls in Venice. His students were so talented that people would travel long distances to hear them perform the music that Vivaldi wrote for them.

Unlike other Baroque composers, Vivaldi did not compose for solo keyboard. However, he was a master of the concerto form (he composed about 500) and is often called the "Father of the Concerto." Vivaldi also wrote sonatas, operas and choral music for the church. He helped popularize the three-movement concerto, which influenced the work of later composers such as Haydn, Mozart and Beethoven.

For many years of his life, Vivaldi enjoyed popularity as a composer; he even worked for royalty all over Europe. At the end of his life, however, he lost his fame and died a poor man. He was buried in a pauper's grave and much of his music was forgotten. Over 100 years later, musicians discovered arrangements of Vivaldi's music that had been done by Johann Sebastian Bach when he was just a boy. And almost 200 years after Vivaldi's death, most of his manuscripts—which had been hidden away in a private collection—were rediscovered. Both the Bach arrangements and the newly found manuscripts renewed Vivaldi's popularity, making him once again a favorite composer from the Baroque era.

Spring Word Search

Using the list in the cloud, look down, across and diagonally to find the words hidden in the puzzle. Circle the words.

```
V U N B A R O Q U E T P
I F W X C V I L D I S R
L H A Y O R P Y J M V I
M T Q U F D G O I R I E
O R P H A N A G E V O S
C O N T I S L H B M L T
O R K E V I V A L D I F
N C O N C E R T O P N S
S P R I N G N B H M A E
P F B U R D S I J Y N A
W O I A L K M G C A L S
E A R T H Q U A K E Z O
F L D O V B A R O X I N
K U S C E H Y J W N G S
```

PRIEST

BAROQUE POEM

CONCERTO VIOLIN ORPHANAGE

SPRING EARTHQUAKE

VIVALDI SEASONS VENICE BIRDS

Spring

(First Movement)

Antonio Vivaldi (1678–1741)
Arr. Carol Matz

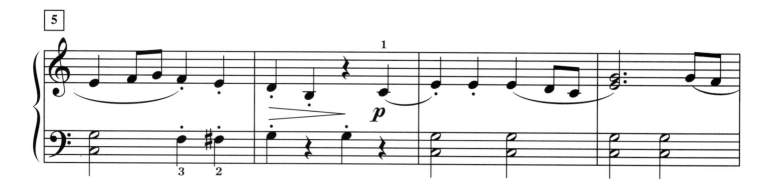

Eine Kleine Nachtmusik

Serenade No. 13 in G Major

for Strings, K. 525

Composer: **Wolfgang Amadeus Mozart**

First Performed: **1787 in Vienna, Austria**

Form: **Serenade**

About the Music

Eine Kleine Nachtmusik means "a little night music." There is no existing information about why the piece was composed or about its first performance. It is simply dated "August 10, 1787," in Mozart's handwriting.

This work was written for a small chamber ensemble of two violins, a viola, a cello and an optional bass. Today, it is most often performed with multiple musicians playing each part. Although it is performed in four movements, *Eine Kleine Nachtmusik* originally had five movements. The original second movement is now lost. The pages of the original manuscript are numbered in a way that suggests the missing movement was torn out of the book. Albert Einstein, who was a great Mozart scholar, suspected that one of Mozart's minuets for piano might actually be a transcription of this missing movement.

Eine Kleine Nachtmusik is one of Mozart's most famous compositions and is probably the best-known serenade of all time. Even though the composition is quite cheerful, surprisingly it was written during a very sad period in Mozart's life— a time when he was recovering from a serious illness and only two months after his father's death.

About the Form

SERENADE

The term *serenade* originally referred to a song played under a girl's balcony by an admirer. *Sera* is Italian for "evening." A serenade is a piece of music intended for evening performance in the open air. In the 18th century, composers started using the term to refer to a suite of lighthearted pieces, often written for a small number of strings and wind instruments.

About the Composer

WOLFGANG AMADEUS MOZART (1756–1791)

Mozart was born in Salzburg, Austria, and grew up in a musical family. His father was an accomplished musician, but found it difficult to teach Mozart music because he seemed to know everything already! Mozart composed his first music when he was only five years old, and by the time he was six, he was giving concerts all over Europe with his sister, Nannerl, playing for kings and queens. By age seven, he could play the keyboard blindfolded, play any music at sight, and create variations on a melody in many different styles. He wrote his first symphony at age nine and his first opera at age twelve. Besides music, Mozart also loved math, and he covered tablecloths and wallpaper with rows of numbers. He also liked animals, and sent the family dog letters from all over Europe when he traveled.

Mozart had the amazing ability to memorize a piece of music after hearing it only once. He played many instruments and composed in every musical form, including symphonies, concertos, operas, songs, masses and chamber music. "Composing is less tiring than doing nothing," he said. He would write down musical ideas wherever he was, on any paper he could find. Often, he would work out a piece of music in his mind as he went about his day's activities and would later sit down to write out what was in his head. Mozart wrote over 600 compositions. His greatest works are

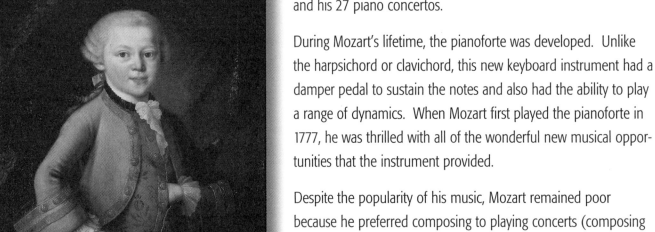

considered to be his 41 symphonies, several of his operas, and his 27 piano concertos.

During Mozart's lifetime, the pianoforte was developed. Unlike the harpsichord or clavichord, this new keyboard instrument had a damper pedal to sustain the notes and also had the ability to play a range of dynamics. When Mozart first played the pianoforte in 1777, he was thrilled with all of the wonderful new musical opportunities that the instrument provided.

Despite the popularity of his music, Mozart remained poor because he preferred composing to playing concerts (composing paid very little), he didn't know how to manage his money very well, and he was very generous with others (often giving away much of what he had). He was only 35 when he died from kidney failure and malnutrition. To this day, the exact location of his grave is unknown.

Eine Kleine Nachtmusik MATCHING Game

Draw a line to connect the star to the matching moon.

Eine Kleine Nachtmusik

(First Movement)

Wolfgang Amadeus Mozart (1756–1791)
Arr. Carol Matz

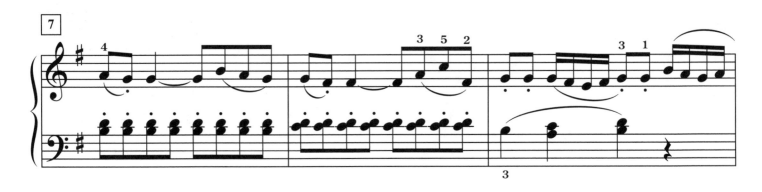

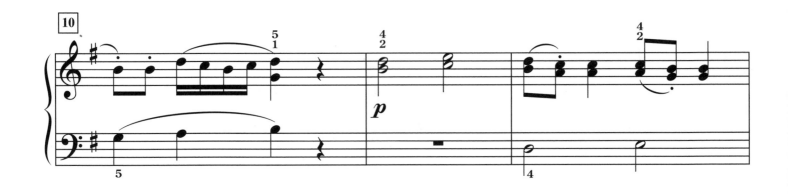

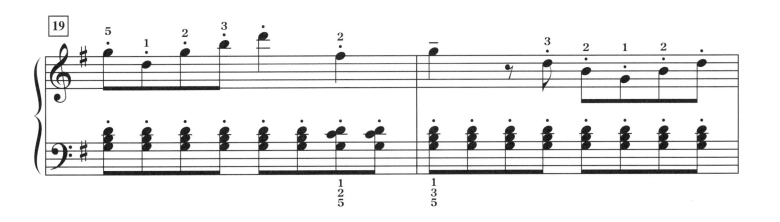

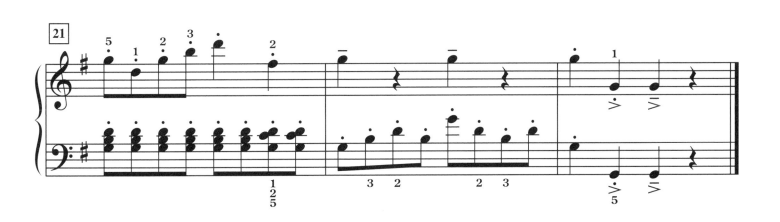

"Surprise" Symphony

Symphony No. 94 in G Major

Composer: **Franz Joseph Haydn**

First Performed: **1792 in London, England**

Form: **Symphony**

About the Music

Haydn's music publishers and friends added nicknames to many of his symphonies. *Symphony No. 94* is nicknamed the "Surprise" Symphony because of the sudden, loud chord that surprises the audience in the middle of the second movement's quiet melody. Haydn had noticed that audiences tended to fall asleep when the music was slow or quiet, so he wrote a full-orchestra crash to wake them up! The "Surprise" Symphony has the traditional four movements of the Classical period. It was written in 1791 and was first performed in London in 1792 with Haydn leading the orchestra. The symphony became instantly popular. When Haydn wrote his oratorio *The Seasons* in 1801, he wove the popular second-movement theme from the "Surprise" Symphony into an aria (solo) sung by the bass. The soloist portrays a farmer who is whistling Haydn's tune as he works.

Following are some nicknames given to other symphonies of Haydn:

"Morning" (No. 6)—it begins with the idea of a sunrise.

"The Farewell" Symphony (No. 45)—the players left the stage one by one during the performance, blowing out candles on their music stands.

"Maria Theresa" (No. 48)—written for a visit by the empress to the Esterhazy Palace.

"The Hen" (No. 83)—a clucking noise is heard in the first movement.

"The Miracle" (No. 96)—the ceiling fell when it was first performed, but no one was injured.

"The Clock" (No. 101)—a comical "tick-tock" bassoon accompaniment is heard in the second movement.

About the Form

SYMPHONY

One of the best-known forms of orchestral music is the *symphony*, a lengthy composition that contains several movements. Classical symphonies—such as those written by Haydn—have the same form (outline) as a sonata, and often contain four movements. An example of the four movements of a Classical symphony follows:

First movement: Allegro (fast tempo)

Second movement: Adagio (slow tempo)

Third movement: Minuet with Trio (medium tempo)

Fourth movement: Finale (fast tempo)

About the Composer

FRANZ JOSEPH HAYDN (1732–1809)

Born in Austria, Franz Joseph Haydn was one of 12 children in a family that loved to sing together in the evenings. At the age of five, Franz was sent to live with a relative near Vienna, which was an important center of music at that time. At the age of seven, he was invited to join the boys' choir of the very important St. Stephen's Cathedral in Vienna, where he not only studied singing, harpsichord and violin, but also heard some of the finest music of the time. At 17, when he left the choir, he only had three old shirts, one coat and no money. For several years, he made hardly any money, trying to support himself by teaching, composing and performing.

When he was 29, Haydn's life changed for the better. He was hired to work as the music director for Prince Esterhazy, a wealthy Hungarian who had some of the finest palaces in Europe. The prince entertained frequently and needed music for his elaborate parties and daily concerts. Haydn had to compose music, direct an orchestra, hire musicians and write out all the orchestra parts by hand. He stayed with the Esterhazy family for 29 years and became famous all over Europe.

Although Haydn was 24 years older than Mozart, the two were friends who greatly admired each other's music. Mozart called Haydn "Papa" and Haydn called him "My Mozart." Mozart once sent Haydn six string quartets he had dedicated to him, along with a note that said, "I send my six sons to you."

Haydn is often called the "Father of the Symphony" since he composed over 100 symphonies and developed the form of the four-movement symphony. He composed in all musical forms of his day, including 25 concertos and nearly 60 keyboard sonatas. By the time Haydn died in 1809, he had become recognized as the greatest living composer.

The Palace at Eszterháza, Hungary, where Haydn was employed.

"Surprise" Symphony Scramble

Unscramble the letters to spell words that complete each sentence.

Then unscramble the circled letters to discover the mystery word. Write it in the percussion instruments.
Hint: Symphony No. 94 in G Major is nicknamed the "_____" Symphony.

1. A symphony has several __ __ __◯__ __ __ __ . **(VMESOTMNE)**

2. Haydn was born in __◯__ __ __ __ __ . **(SRATAIU)**

3. Haydn sang in the boys' choir at St. ◯__ __ __ __ __ __ ' __ Cathedral. **(TESHESPN)**

4. Haydn worked for __◯__ __ __ __ Esterhazy. **(CRENIP)**

5. __◯__ __ __ __ __ __ __ were given to many of Haydn's symphonies. **(INANKMSEC)**

6. Mozart gave Haydn the name of "◯__ __ __" . **(AAPP)**

7. Haydn is often called the " __ __ __ __ __◯ of the symphony". **(HTFAER)**

8. The second movement of Symphony No. 94 has a ◯__ __ __ __ __ , loud chord. **(DNSUED)**

Mystery Word:

Theme from the
"Surprise" Symphony
(Second Movement)

Franz Joseph Haydn (1732–1809)
Arr. Carol Matz

Moderately

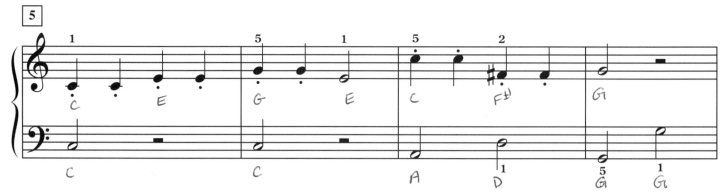

Symphony No. 5

in C Minor

Composer: **Ludwig van Beethoven**

First Performed: **1808 in Vienna, Austria**

Form: **Symphony**

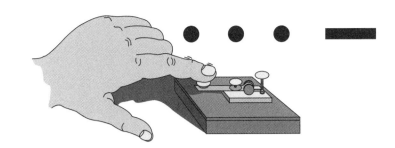

About the Music

Beethoven's *Symphony No. 5* was first performed in Vienna, Austria, on December 22, 1808, when Beethoven was 38 years old. It was the opening piece for the second half of an all-Beethoven concert that Beethoven conducted. The concert was four hours long, so by the time the *Symphony No. 5* was played, the audience was too tired to pay much attention. Also, they were nearly frozen since the performance hall was unheated and the weather was extremely cold! This first performance was poor because the orchestra had only one rehearsal before the concert. At one point, the players became so confused that Beethoven had to stop and restart the music. About a year and a half later, the symphony finally began to win audience approval.

This symphony took Beethoven several years to complete. It opens with probably the four best-known notes in classical music: three short notes and one long note. This musical idea is heard in various ways in all four movements of the symphony. *Symphony No. 5* became even more famous during World War II because the rhythm of the opening four notes is the same as Morse code for the letter "V" (short-short-short-long), which was the signal for "victory" whenever the Allied forces triumphed on the battlefield.

Beethoven's *Symphony No. 5*, which may be the most celebrated symphony of all time, is a good representative of the passion and intensity of the Romantic style of music. In a review from 1810, E. T. A. Hoffmann called this symphony "one of the most important works of the age."

About the Form

SYMPHONY

A symphony is a long composition for orchestra, written in several movements, each with a different tempo, style, or mood that contrasts with the others. The four movements of Beethoven's Symphony No. 5 are as follows:

First movement: Allegro con brio

Second movement: Andante con moto (in the form of a theme and variations)

Third movement: Allegro (in the form of a *scherzo*—a quick, playful movement that Beethoven used instead of the typical *minuet*)

Fourth movement: Allegro

About the Composer

LUDWIG VAN BEETHOVEN (1770–1827)

Beethoven was born in Bonn, Germany in 1770. Like Bach and Mozart, he came from a musical family. When he was four, he started lessons in piano, violin and composition with his father. He admired the music of Mozart, Clementi and Haydn (with whom he studied briefly). By the time he was 13, he had published compositions. When he was 22, he moved to Vienna where he spent the rest of his life performing, composing and teaching.

Beethoven's music is a bridge between the Classical and Romantic periods. The music of the Classical period was sometimes not overly serious, but Beethoven had a powerful personality that poured out of his music as he expressed his personal struggles and emotions, unlike any composer before him.

Beethoven became one of the most talented composers and performers in all of Europe. His performances on the piano were wild, filled with wrong notes, broken hammers and strings, and more emotion than audiences were used to hearing or seeing. Early in his career, he was such a well-known pianist that few recognized he was a talented composer. In 1809, the Austrian royalty signed an agreement to give Beethoven a lifetime salary so that he could stay in Vienna and devote himself to composing. He was always up early, composing several hours before breakfast.

Among his compositions are numerous orchestral pieces, oratorios, songs, 32 piano sonatas, 5 piano concertos and 9 symphonies. Beethoven loved nature and took two long walks daily. His walks in the country inspired him to compose many of his masterpieces, including *Symphony No. 6* (nicknamed the "Pastorale") in which one can hear birds singing, a waterfall and a thunderstorm. Beethoven added new instruments to the orchestra such as the trombone. He even added a chorus of voices for his *Symphony No. 9*, something never done before.

When he was 29, Beethoven began to lose his hearing. He had written only two of his nine symphonies by this time. There were many painful events in his life because of his increasing deafness, such as getting lost while conducting the orchestra and losing his ability to perform. Though he was often depressed about his condition, he wrote some of his greatest works in total deafness, remembering the sounds of the notes in his head.

When Beethoven died at age 57, he was a hero. Varied reports say that between ten to thirty thousand people attended his funeral. Beethoven never married, but after his death, his friends found letters to someone he called his "immortal beloved."

Symphony No. 5

Puzzle

Draw a line through the incorrect answer.

1. Beethoven's Symphony (*No. 5/No. 9*) uses a chorus of voices.

2. Symphony No. 5 became a signal for (*defeat/victory*) during World War II.

3. Beethoven added the (*trumpet/trombone*) to the orchestra.

4. Beethoven suffered from (*blindness/deafness*).

5. Beethoven was born in (*Austria/Germany*) in (*1770/1870*).

6. His music is a bridge between the (*Baroque and Classical/Classical and Romantic*) periods of music.

7. Symphony No. 5 was first performed in (*Vienna/Bonn*).

8. A symphony is a (*short/long*) composition for orchestra in several (*movements/acts*).

Beethoven's birthplace in Bonn as it is today

Symphony No. 5

(First Movement)

Ludwig van Beethoven (1770–1827)
Arr. Carol Matz

Morning Mood

from "Peer Gynt Suite"

Composer: **Edvard Grieg**

First Performed: **1876 in Oslo, Norway**

Form: **Suite**

About the Music

In 1874, Norwegian playwright Henrik Ibsen asked Grieg to write music for his new play, *Peer Gynt*. Grieg wrote 22 compositions for the play, for which he received about $200. He thought composing the music would be easy, but it ended up taking him two years to complete the job. Grieg's music was an important reason why the play became so popular, and led to Grieg's fame as a composer. The first performance of *Peer Gynt* took place in 1876 and was a huge success.

Peer Gynt is the story of a boy named Peer (Norwegian for "Peter") who travels the world and has many adventures, which often get him into trouble. Eventually, he returns home to Norway—older and wiser— and returns to his sweetheart, Solveig. Grieg's music for the play reflects many different emotions and paints a picture of Peer Gynt's adventures. "Morning Mood," one of the pieces from *Peer Gynt*, is a quiet and peaceful composition that represents a sunrise. The orchestral version begins with a beautiful flute melody, suggesting a bird singing at dawn. It was written for Act IV of the play when, during his adventures, Peer wakes up in an Arabian desert only to find out he has been robbed of everything.

Grieg created two orchestral suites (groups of pieces) from the complete score and later transcribed them for piano. Along with "Morning Mood," some of the most performed selections from the suites are "In the Hall of the Mountain King," "Anitra's Dance," and "Solveig's Song."

About the Form

SUITE

The term "suite" originated in the 1500s, referring to several dance movements following one another. Over time, this instrumental form evolved as a collection of orchestral pieces taken from a longer work such as a ballet (Tchaikovsky's *Nutcracker Suite*), opera, or play (Grieg's *Peer Gynt Suite*). Pieces from orchestral suites are performed without any dancing or singing.

About the Composer

EDVARD GRIEG (1843–1907)

Edvard Grieg was born in Bergen, Norway and began studying piano at age six. His first teacher was his mother, who was known as the best piano teacher in Bergen. He fell in love with music while listening to her play Mozart, Beethoven and Chopin. Young Edvard did not like to practice his lessons and preferred to spend his time experimenting with new sounds and chords. At age nine, he composed his first piece, a set of variations on a Norwegian folk melody.

When Grieg was 15, he attended the Leipzig Conservatory in Germany to study with some of the finest piano teachers in Europe. While in Leipzig, Grieg had the chance to hear Robert Schumann's *Piano Concerto in A Minor* performed by the composer's wife, Clara Schumann. This performance inspired Grieg to write his own *Piano Concerto in A Minor*, one of his most famous works and one of the most frequently performed concertos.

Portrait of Greig accompanying his wife Nina, by P. S. Krøer

After finishing school, Grieg began to perform in Norway. He then spent several years in Denmark where he married his cousin Nina, a talented singer. Grieg's vocal composition "I Love Thee" was given to Nina as an engagement present. Nina often performed with Grieg in recitals, singing his songs and playing piano duets. Grieg became a well-known teacher and conductor. He also founded the Norwegian Academy of Music in Oslo (1866) so that Norwegian students could receive a good musical education without having to leave the country.

Among Grieg's compositions are vocal pieces, works for chorus and orchestra, a string quartet, a piano concerto, and the music for *Peer Gynt*. A nationalist composer, Grieg was very interested in the history and songs of his native Norway. Many of his compositions were influenced by the folk music and legends that he heard in his childhood. Grieg spent his life promoting and supporting his country's music and performing pieces mostly by Norwegian composers. He became one of the most well-known figures in Norway, and upon his death he was honored with a state funeral.

Peer Gynt Suite

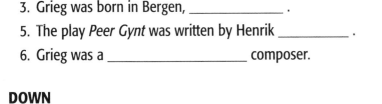

Complete the sentences below, then write the answers in the crossword puzzle. Choose your answers from the given words.

Norwegian fjord

ACROSS

2. Edvard _____ was born in 1843.

3. Grieg was born in Bergen, _____ .

5. The play *Peer Gynt* was written by Henrik _____ .

6. Grieg was a _____ composer.

DOWN

1. Grieg wrote music for the play _____ _____ .

3. The composer married his cousin _____ .

4. " _____ _____ " is a song from *Peer Gynt*.

7. Grieg's *Piano* _____ *in A Minor* is one of his most famous compositions.

8. A _____ is a collection of orchestral pieces.

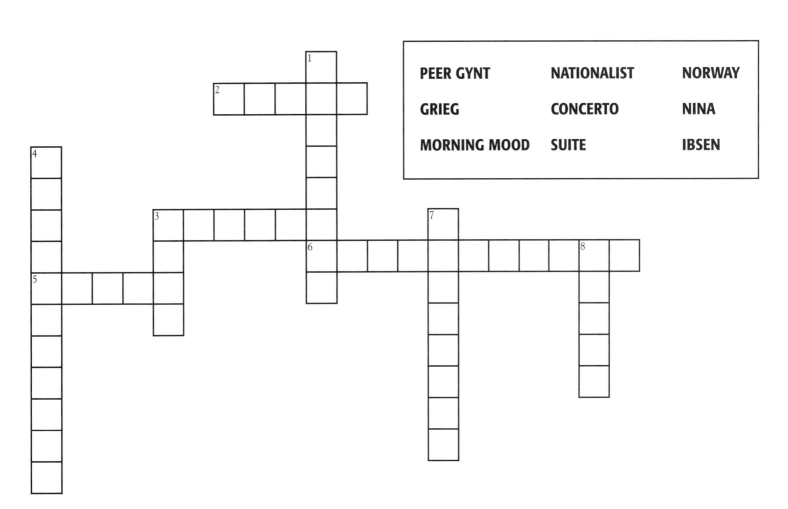

PEER GYNT	NATIONALIST	NORWAY
GRIEG	CONCERTO	NINA
MORNING MOOD	SUITE	IBSEN

Morning Mood

Edvard Grieg (1843–1907)
Arr. Carol Matz

1812 Overture

Composer: **Peter Ilyich Tchaikovsky**

First Performed: **1882 in Moscow, Russia**

Form: **Overture**

About the Music

The *1812 Overture* is one of Tchaikovsky's most famous orchestral compositions. It was written to celebrate the 70th anniversary of the Russian victory over Napoleon's French army in 1812. When Tchaikovsky came to the United States in 1891, he conducted the piece at the dedication of Carnegie Hall in New York City.

Tchaikovsky's famous overture is *program music*—a composition that tells a story or paints a picture. The opening theme is based on the Russian hymn "Save Us, O Lord," which recalls the declaration of war announced during church services in Russia. After the opening theme, parts of the French tune "La Marseillaise" are heard, representing Napoleon's French troops. This tune is then followed by a Russian folk song. The close of the overture, featuring bells and live cannons firing, announces the liberation of Moscow. However, this musical depiction is much more dramatic than what really happened— Napoleon and his men were actually defeated by starvation and Russia's bitterly cold winter.

Tchaikovsky himself confessed that he found his overture "very noisy." He intended the *1812 Overture* to be played outdoors with the ringing of church bells, fireworks displays, and live cannons firing (a booming bass drum is often substituted for the live cannon blasts). When the Boston Pops Orchestra performs the *1812 Overture* each Fourth of July, real cannon fire is used along with a huge fireworks show.

About the Form

OVERTURE

Overture comes from the French word *ouverture*, which means "opening." Many overtures are instrumental compositions written to introduce a large work such as an opera or ballet. Some of these overtures have become so well known that they are performed in concert on their own (for example, Rossini's *William Tell Overture*). An overture may also be a composition that is written to describe a particular event (Tchaikovsky's *1812 Overture*) or strong emotions (Brahms' *Tragic Overture*).

Carnegie Hall in 1891

About the Composer

PETER ILYICH TCHAIKOVSKY (1840–1893)

Peter Ilyich Tchaikovsky is one of the most well-known Russian composers. Because of his orchestral music and ballets, he was the first Russian composer to attain worldwide popularity.

Even as a young child, Tchaikovsky loved music. His parents encouraged him to develop his talent, but they did not encourage him to pursue music as a career; instead, they wanted him to be a lawyer. Tchaikovsky graduated from law school and worked for the government, but after a short time, he enrolled in the St. Petersburg Conservatory to study music seriously. After graduation, he was immediately given a job as a teacher at the Moscow Conservatory.

Tchaikovsky wrote six symphonies, orchestral suites, concertos, piano music, and operas. However, he is probably best remembered for his three ballets: *Swan Lake, The Sleeping Beauty* and *The Nutcracker*. It is said that *The Nutcracker Suite* (containing six selections from the ballet) has interested more people in classical music than any other music in history. Sadly, none of Tchaikovsky's ballets were very successful during his lifetime. In addition to becoming a world-famous composer, Tchaikovsky was also a great conductor, teacher of composition and music critic.

Tchaikovsky's masterpieces might never have been written without the help of a mysterious and wealthy woman named Ma dame von Meck. A great lover of music, she became Tchaikovsky's greatest financial and musical supporter. For 13 years, she gave Tchaikovsky money so that he could leave his teaching position at the conservatory and devote himself entirely to composing. However, she insisted that they never meet in person.

Tchaikovsky's last work, which he considered his best, was his *Symphony No. 6* (the "Pathetique"). Tchaikovsky died soon after its first performance, and it was played at his funeral service.

Swan position from Swan Lake

1812 Overture

Using the code at the bottom of the page, fill in the blanks.

"Overture" is a French word meaning ___ ___ ___ ___ ___ ___ ___.
15 16 5 14 9 14 7

The *1812 Overture* was written to use real ___ ___ ___ ___ ___ ___ ___ at the end of the piece.
3 1 14 14 15 14 19

Tchaikovsky wanted the overture to be played ___ ___ ___ ___ ___ ___ ___ ___ , using
15 21 20 4 15 15 18 19

ringing ___ ___ ___ ___ ___ ___ ___ ___ ___ ___ ___ and ___ ___ ___ ___ ___ ___ ___ ___ ___.
3 8 21 18 3 8 — 2 5 12 12 19 — 6 9 18 5 23 15 18 11 19

Many overtures were written to ___ ___ ___ ___ ___ ___ ___ ___ ___ a larger work such as an opera or a ballet.
9 14 20 18 15 4 21 3 5

___ ___ ___ ___ ___ ___ ___ ___ ___ ___ ___ is one of the best-known ___ ___ ___ ___ ___ ___ ___ composers.
20 3 8 1 9 11 15 22 19 11 25 — 18 21 19 19 9 1 14

Tchaikovsky composed six ___ ___ ___ ___ ___ ___ ___ ___ ___ ___ but is best remembered
19 25 13 16 8 15 14 9 5 19

for his three ___ ___ ___ ___ ___ ___ ___ .
2 1 12 12 5 20 19

NUMBER CODE:

A.........1	N.........14
B.........2	O.........15
C.........3	P.........16
D.........4	Q.........17
E.........5	R.........18
F.........6	S.........19
G.........7	T.........20
H.........8	U.........21
I.........9	V.........22
J.........10	W.........23
K.........11	X.........24
L.........12	Y.........25
M.........13	Z.........26

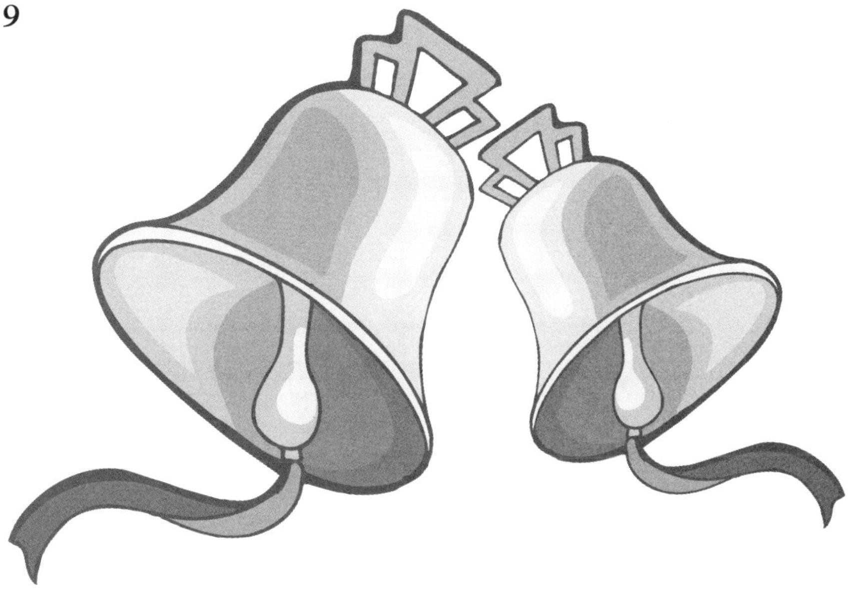

48

Theme from

1812 Overture

Peter Ilyich Tchaikovsky (1840–1893)
Arr. Carol Matz

Moderately fast

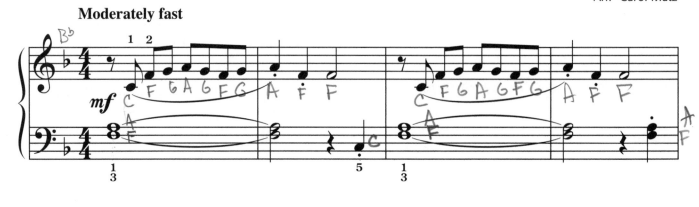

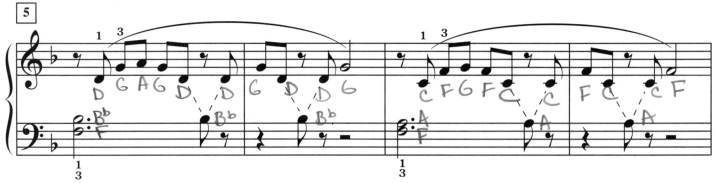

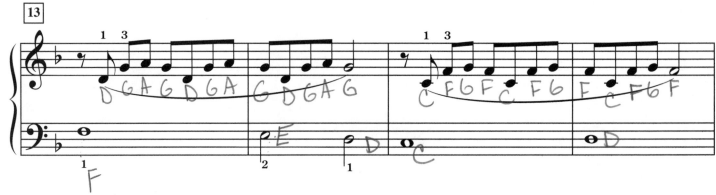

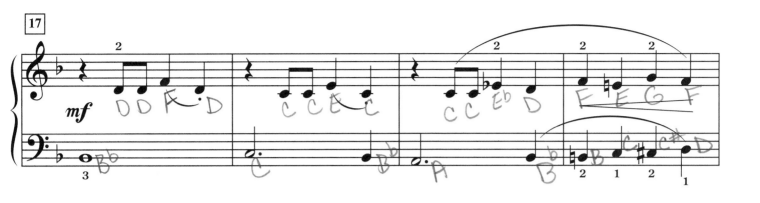

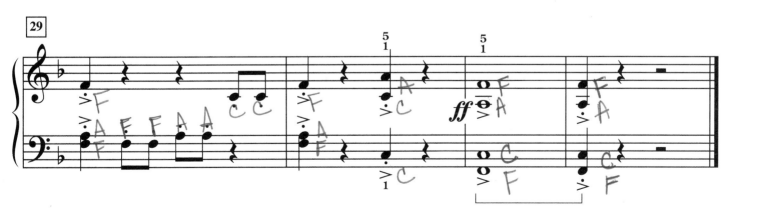

50

Rhapsody in Blue™

Composer: **George Gershwin**

First Performed: **1924 in New York City**

Form: **Concerto in the form of a "Rhapsody"**

About the Music

Rhapsody in Blue, written in 1924, was one of the first compositions to combine symphonic music and jazz. Gershwin was only 25 years old when conductor Paul Whiteman asked him to write a jazz-style concerto for an upcoming New York concert called "An Experiment in Modern Music." Gershwin composed Rhapsody in Blue in only three weeks because he had forgotten about the project until he saw a newspaper ad for the upcoming concert. Things were so rushed at the first performance that the orchestra parts were still being written-out as the audience entered the auditorium! After the performance, Gershwin received a standing ovation from the huge audience, which included composers Sergei Rachmaninoff and Igor Stravinsky.

When Rhapsody in Blue was originally published, the editors removed 88 measures of music to try to make the piece sound more "classical." It wasn't until 1996, after the original manuscript was discovered, that the piece was finally published as George Gershwin first wrote it. Today, Rhapsody in Blue is one of the most frequently performed orchestral works by an American composer.

About the Form

Rhapsody in Blue is a piano concerto (piano plus orchestra) written in the style of a rhapsody.

RHAPSODY

Rhapsody comes from the Greek word rhapsoidia, which literally means "songs stitched together." A rhapsody has a free style, with no particular musical form. The term began to be used frequently in the 19th century, describing long compositions in which different ideas— sometimes taken from folk songs—were strung together (for example Liszt's Hungarian Rhapsody).

About the Composer

GEORGE GERSHWIN (1898–1937)

As a young boy in Brooklyn, New York, George Gershwin was more interested in baseball and roller-skating than he was in music. But around the age of 10, he heard a student play the violin at a school assembly and became fascinated with music. He started to pick out tunes and make up melodies on a piano that belonged to his older brother Ira, until finally his parents let him take piano lessons. At age 16, he became a "song plugger," playing and singing other composers' songs for the customers in local music stores, earning $15 a week. All the while, he was writing his own popular tunes, and by the time he was 19, several had been published. His song *Swanee*, recorded when he was 21, earned $100,000 its first year.

George and Ira Gershwin became a famous songwriting team, with George writing the music and Ira supplying the words. Together they created popular songs, Broadway shows, and music for movies. The brothers were very close and even lived in neighboring apartments.

George also composed many works without Ira. He wrote pianos concertos (*Rhapsody in Blue*, *Concerto in F*), a set of piano preludes, orchestral works (*An American in Paris*, *Cuban Overture*), and one opera (*Porgy and Bess*).

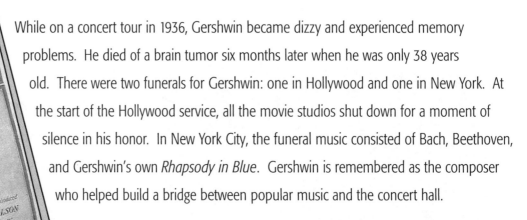

While on a concert tour in 1936, Gershwin became dizzy and experienced memory problems. He died of a brain tumor six months later when he was only 38 years old. There were two funerals for Gershwin: one in Hollywood and one in New York. At the start of the Hollywood service, all the movie studios shut down for a moment of silence in his honor. In New York City, the funeral music consisted of Bach, Beethoven, and Gershwin's own *Rhapsody in Blue*. Gershwin is remembered as the composer who helped build a bridge between popular music and the concert hall.

Rhapsody in Blue™

Fill in the blanks using the list of words below.

1. *Rhapsody in Blue* combines symphonic music and _____ .

2. The song _____ earned Gershwin $100,000 when he was 21.

3. George's favorite writing partner was _____ , his brother.

4. *Rhapsody in Blue* was written in _____ weeks.

5. The Gershwin brothers were also well-known for writing _____ shows.

6. _____ means "songs stitched together" and is written in a _____ style.

7. *Rhapsody in Blue* is a piano _____ because it is a piece for piano and orchestra.

8. Gershwin was born in _____ _____ .

9. Two famous composers, _____ and _____ , were in the audience for the first performance of *Rhapsody in Blue.*

FREE
IRA
CONCERTO
BROADWAY
RHAPSODY
STRAVINSKY
RACHMANINOFF
JAZZ
NEW YORK
SWANEE
THREE

Themes from

Rhapsody in Blue™

By George Gershwin (1898–1937)
Arr. Carol Matz

Glossary of Musical Terms

Arrangement The re-writing of a composition that adapts the original for different instruments.

Baroque period 1600–1750. Major composers: J.S. Bach, Handel, Vivaldi

Classical period 1750–1820. Major composers: Haydn, Mozart, Beethoven

Concerto A composition for solo instrument plus orchestra.

Form The outline of a composition.

Impressionist Referring to the period of music known as Impressionism (1890–1910). Major composers: Debussy, Ravel, Satie

Improvisation The spontaneous creation of music while it is being performed.

Jazz A style of American music that developed in the early 20th century. Jazz has its roots in blues and ragtime, and usually features improvisation.

Manuscript An original copy of a composer's handwritten music.

Movement A section or part of a larger musical work.

Nationalist A composer who expresses pride in his or her country by using traditional folk tunes, stories, and instruments.

Oratorio A composition for orchestra and voices, based on a religious story.

Program music Music that suggests visual ideas, usually "depicting" a story, scene, poem, or event.

Romantic period 1820–1910. Major composers: Beethoven, Schubert, Schumann, Mendelssohn, Tchaikovsky

Section leader The leader of an orchestral section (strings, woodwinds, brass, or percussion).

Symphony A multi-movement composition for orchestra.

Transcription A composition that has been written out for different instruments or voices than originally intended.

Variations Repetitions of a musical theme, which have been modified through such elements as rhythm, melody, tempo, mood, or harmony.